A Reminder of Hunger and Wings

poems by

Jane Ebihara

Finishing Line Press
Georgetown, Kentucky

A Reminder of Hunger and Wings

Copyright © 2019 by Jane Ebihara
ISBN 978-1-63534-835-4 First Edition
All rights reserved under International and Pan-American Copyright Conventions. No part of this book may be reproduced in any manner whatsoever without written permission from the publisher, except in the case of brief quotations embodied in critical articles and reviews.

ACKNOWLEDGMENTS

Grateful acknowledgment is made to the following publications in which some of the poems in this collection first appeared:

The Doll Anthology (Terrapin Press 2016) "The Milk House"
The Donut Anthology (Terrapin Press 2017) "Portrait"
Dandelion Review (2016) "The Day After You Died"
The *Stillwater Review* (2014) "The Poet Watches a Spider"
The *Stillwater Review* (2018) "To the Doe Nursing Her Fawn in the Middle of the Road"
Tiferet (2017) "Dying in Autumn" "Morning Still"
Tiferet (2018) "Life Still"
U.S. 1 Worksheets (2015) "Poem in Flight"
U.S. I Worksheets (2018) " After Tutoring"
Voices From Here II (2017) "Lesson from the Moon;" "Night Walk"

Publisher: Leah Maines
Editor: Christen Kincaid
Cover Art: Jean LeBlanc
Author Photo: Jane Ebihara
Cover Design: Leah Huete

Printed in the USA on acid-free paper.
Order online: www.finishinglinepress.com
also available on amazon.com

Author inquiries and mail orders:
Finishing Line Press
P. O. Box 1626
Georgetown, Kentucky 40324
U. S. A.

Table of Contents

First Memory 1

Roots 2

Portrait 3

The Day After You Died.. 4

The Milk House 5

November Gardener 6

This Story Could Be True 7

In Search of a Poem... 8

Night Walk 9

To the Doe Nursing Her Fawn in the Middle of the Road............ 10

Listening to a Distant Thunder 11

The Poet Watches a Spider 12

Poem in Flight.. 13

Muse in Winter Light 14

Almost April... 15

April Frost.. 16

Betrayal 17

Dying in Autumn 18

The Lie... 19

What the Dreamer Knows.. 20

Eight Months Gone 21

Morning Still.. 22

Waking Widowed 24

A New Season 25

After Tutoring 27

Lesson from the Moon.. 28

Life Still... 29

for my family

First Memory

at age two
she stands in a field
of cosmos bloom
and looks up

hypnotized
by lacy light-play
through pastel
petals

she hears her mother call
but stands
still as stone

her first memory
this one
of quiet rebellion

Roots

she was from

barefoot summers
firefly nights
birdsong   rainwater

and silence

a man who loved morning
a swing in the walnut tree
breakfast on a camp stove

and Little Lulu

a woman
who loved herself
pull up your socks
what would people think

and grandma next door

smocked pinafores
saddle shoes and
pot roast on Sundays

she was from
daydreams and yearning
to be from somewhere
else

Portrait

my grandmother
a quiet woman
      had fine thin hair combed to below her waist
      then braided and wound around her head
a deserved crown

to allow a man to see her bare feet would not be proper
she washed her hair in rainwater
loved God and Will Rogers

she made handstitched quilts with remnants
      of cotton housedresses
made dinner from jars of canned carrots tomatoes corn and peas
      that lined the cellar shelves
snapped beans straight from her garden
      into the hammock of her hand-sewn apron and
        made milk warm for kittens in the smokehouse
and she made donuts

with yeast and flour butter sugar nutmeg
and eggs lifted fresh from beneath the hen
she mixed   measured   melted   and beat
      let rise to double the size
then cut and fried
      tossed them in a paper bag of sugar

my grandmother didn't make a man leave her
he did that alone
he alone turned his back on everything warm she once held
everything she raised in his absence

The Day After You Died

Mother
my plane lowers over Chicago
after the snow

the tiny window
cools my forehead

below
the world is black and white
I'm supposed to be remembering
I'm supposed to weep

you have already been fed to the flame
gone up with unlikely passion

now my rental car slices a dark line
through Midwest farmland

what strange familiarity
this place
where you no longer live
where I no longer live

snow squalls throw ashen showers
onto the blurred windshield
wipers drone
it's late   too late   too late

I might slide off this road remembering
be found by locals
who'd say *she's a stranger here*
we'll have to see where she came from

it's late   too late   too late

The Milk House

after the town swelled
swallowed the farms in its path
the abandoned milk house
dark but for one small window
sat solid   useless
at the end of our gravel drive

I moved in   I was six
apple crate cupboard   terry towel on the window
rag rug to cover the cold cement
wicker basket for my doll

for a different child this shelter might have been
a clubhouse   a place to hide   to brood
for me a nest where
if I stood on tiptoe at the window
I could watch the gardener next door
tend to her young

I gathered chickweed and dandelion
to nourish my babe
I swaddled   sang   soothed
until each blue eye closed
with a tiny click

I was not neighborly
no imaginary husband
clattered about   I was content
alone with my child

still on occasion
a visitor knocked   stooped to enter

one who thought I should know
my baby would melt if
I left her too long in the sun

November Gardener

she likes flowers whose names
remind her of young girls
no one wants to play with
Cleome   Acacia   Calantha   Helenium

her fingers move
light as wingbeats
through garden bounty
search for beauty now spent

she touches
the finished and the flaming
with equal tenderness

runs her thumb and forefinger
down the fading stem until she finds
just the right place to
free the now brittle bloom

it's coming she knows
winters here don't bluff   it's coming
she knows too
these tiny deaths are not omens
but promises

This Story Could Be True

she watches
five jays scrabble
for stale bread
tossed on crusty snow

she sees how they take
more than they can carry
knows they want more
than she has to give

will they bring her a gift these jays
      their corvid kin the crows
         bring things that shine
            paper clips
             pieces of foil

if this story were true
there would be a man too
a man who wants to die
      hoards his pain
      like a rare collection
      fills the house with winter

perhaps what the jays bring
is simply blue   a feather
the color of stormy skies
a reminder of hunger
and wings

In Search of a Poem

she meant to write about the dream
where she was young again   naked
in the arms of a kind and gentle stranger
the dream where she woke with a shudder

she'd once been told that
if she dreamed of falling
she must wake before she
hit the ground   or die

but there was no poem there

she considered the dream
of the night before and thought perhaps…
but then she'd dreamt only of woods
like those outside her window
where craggy trees folded onto the forest floor
                    blocked a once remembered trail
yet
not even the slice of winter light
that stabbed the snowy boughs
could make that a poem

nor could the snoring man beside her
his back turned away

seems the language of dreams
does not always unfold delicate truths
sometimes dreams
simply point
to the place where a path
used to be

Night Walk

when sleep eludes
she imagines a walk

right at the end of the driveway
to the place where she found the newborn fawn
still wet
so still
> *my babies were beautiful too*

and just beyond the curve in the road
where the wild turkey's strut delighted
tail fanned   flamed
in search of love
> *a dangerous gift—desire*

then that stretch of woods where
garbled whispers once revealed a
venue of vultures darkly hunched
huddled on the autumn floor
> *society in shadow*

underfoot
the snap of stems
a foraged garden
> *the night fills with ruin*

To the Doe Nursing Her Fawn in the Middle of the Road

love is no sister to common sense
hunger not even a distant cousin
we mean to be careful mothers
yet have all thrown caution aside
in the name of desire

I have made my own foolish choices
fueled by what wells
swollen and throbbing inside
that which I offered up as devotion

often too
in unlikely places

Listening to a Distant Thunder

oppressive heat lifts on this wind
white pines sway and speak
toss brittle needles at our feet

what is that whispered word

we should know
for we are brittle too
drop barbs of our own
to pierce the air
we breathe

there have been simple signs
things out of place
       that groundhog in the tree
       the tree frog on the window pane
       words that batter like moths

it hesitates now
this summer storm
teases   then falls quiet
still we know it stirs
know it will weigh us down with its magnitude
we know too much malice
will uproot us

storms are like that
       picking things up
       putting them down
       where they don't belong

The Poet Watches a Spider

little weaver
little magician
little acrobat
is it hunger that drives you
to this art
to work without a net
held by a thread

how do you know
where to go next
in your magnificent maze

little dreamer
slave to wind to whim
and we who wipe your
work away
without a thought

little mime
touching the sides
of your invisible world

teach me how to create
such ordered artistry

little spinner
teach me patience

teach me to weave
beauty from nothing

create wonder
from want

Poem in Flight

poets love moths
cannot resist
the ease of metaphor
clamoring as they do toward light

poets love anything fragile
that flings itself into flame

poets love wings
        that navigate in the dark
        seek the desired

and hope this time
nothing will burn

Muse in Winter Light

poems arrive in early light
cling to the empty bellies of deer or

the weakened wings of the dove
with its winter lament

today

the trees are alive with poetry
bare limbs blacken with their arrival

a murmuration of starlings
raucous flourish of confusion

they hesitate   lift

one wildly twisting cloud
a fluid synchrony of flight

then

like a quill dipped in black
they release a whispered secret
across the empty sky

Almost April

what's left of winter

       sullen dirty mounds of what was beauty
       misshapen stakes set to guide the plows
       dismissed carrots thrown to hungry deer
            who roam
                   slack-skinned and hopeful

    you and I
    still here
    watch snow that does not melt
    listen for birdsong
    we cannot hear
    just yet

April Frost

see how the daffodils
lower their heads
like abandoned lovers
bereft of touch
when only yesterday
they thrived on tenderness

such thievery overnight

remember the feverish light
the lingering caress
that lifted your face
to the sun

remember how you thought
it would always be so

Betrayal

damn her
damn you
it was I who carried this embryo of grief
for months before you went to her

your longing had once been
for me—for us
but that was before
before your body betrayed you
trapped you in its warp and wound
disguised itself as villain

before you met your
temptress Death
her dark open arms and
promise to draw you in
let you spill your misery inside her

I gave you everything
you left me only
this now swaddled sorrow

a living thing
hungry and
fully formed

Dying in Autumn

she stands at the window
watches the leaves let go
she thinks
> *color blind he would have seen this autumn day*
> *with its mouth full of gold as gray and grayer*
> *seen shock of sun   shadow of raven*

he would comment perhaps on
stark bare limbs
the beauty of what remains

she watches the silent show
listens for
the sound of his voice

The Lie

They ask: How are you doing?

*the dishwasher's broken I don't wish my mother were here
there's a baby bunny in the lawn I hope it doesn't
get hit by a mower I only sleep well with the windows
open this is my home but I feel like I work here searched
the sky for a rainbow yesterday car needs a new muffler
don't say I am not alone wonder where the mother
rabbit is saw a yellow finch in the dogwood need a good
laugh I don't play the piano well but I can't hear his pain
over "we will never love like this again" I destroyed
his letters long ago*

What the Dreamer Knows

he'd left her months before
though he was not yet gone
when she had the dream

where she walked away
barefoot
in the snow

she knew it was foolish
dangerous
but this snow was soft and warm
felt like sumptuous bedding

she knew she should get out of it
soon
before she was forever crippled

still
she lay in that snow
as if it were a warm white sheet
drawn to her throat

Eight Months Gone

tomorrow
I'll pack the car
for a trip to the Catskills
    take the kids some fresh fruit
    birthday gifts for your son
    and the box of bone and ash
        that is not you

your instructions
mix my ashes with the dogs'
ended there
failed to say   what then

what did you want
    water or woods   petal or fern
        a toss in the wind   or   a turn in the earth

in eighty years you never learned to rest
in forty years I rarely knew what you wanted
still I know
what you would not

the box is wrong

Morning Still

I've given away all your clothes
except that denim shirt
sleeves still rolled by your hand
yet when I hold it to my face
I cannot find you there

the last day
I thought you were drowning
not gasping for air but
inviting the last of it

when the final shudder
let you go
I breathed *there   there*
you found what you wanted

you were small
like a child
when they carried you away
wrapped in a green and white checked sheet
the one we took to the beach for the children's bed

your frame
a brittle empty structure
artifact already

I shouldn't have lifted the sheet
kissed your cold brow
wanted just a little more
time   hope

you began your leaving so long ago
I had already rehearsed widowhood
embraced the silence   the loneliness of singularity
grieved the loss of you
nearly forgotten your touch

morning comes anyway
the day does not care that you are gone

Waking Widowed

four seasons now
still that slap of reality
with each dawn
it is so   it is really so
even my bed a startling
                unfamiliar field

nightmares fade in the day's light
truth does not
widow   I am a widow
the word itself sounds broken

widow the word a printer says
doesn't fit on a page
rests alone on the next
leftover

the widow
something   not someone

in forty years
not once did I wake to the thought
I am married
how many seasons
before I wake without the wound

widows no longer wear black
we wear a different costume
one that feels stolen
from another woman's closet

a gown that falls
heavily on the body
like an unanswered question

which one of us is gone

A New Season

this is not a poem about autumn

though you might guess so if you
saw me writing here
      in quiet woods
        while a soft breeze loosens
           another sycamore leaf

      where squirrels skitter and skeetch
          over mounds of fallen pine needles
          follow a fading memory

this is not a poem about death

      though soon these woods
      will announce the strange
      loveliness of leaving
      with a riot of red and gold

you left me in autumn
you have never left me
both will always be so

this is not a poem about you

I've spread those poems across the endless nights
now I'm weary
of ruin

alone
I am alone
that may always be so

this is not a poem about me

the lake is alive now
sun and wind play on the surface

I am alive
watch a new season arrive

sometimes this
is how
a love poem
ends

After Tutoring

Angie didn't finish high school
so now at forty-five she wants to decode
the mysteries of dependent clauses
appositives   algebra

she'll be a nurse someday she vows
clean her *own* hardwood floors and
at a table by a window
sunlight will stream
onto the pages of her open book
she'll kneel in that house
hands folded in prayer

all this she shares as we cross
the parking lot to go our separate ways
Do you like that? she asks and points above us
where blue clouds curl themselves into
shapes of things imagined best
by children spinning tales

I love looking up she says

Lesson from the Moon

how whole a half can be

half a dream still a dream
half a song lives on
half a meal can satisfy
half a moon shows how
    half a light
is whole enough

Life Still

alone
on this Pennsylvania hillside
I watch layers of mountain and sky share
motionless waves of greens and blues
like some vast unreachable ocean

still life with birdsong
sonorous invitation and response
tossed tree to tree

how many languages do they speak
or is it only one   they
        so much better at brotherhood
        than we

see how that Finch has no fear
of the Phoebe's call

she has her own voice

you're gone for months now
and I am a little less lost each day

if I believed in heaven
I would wish you here

on this hillside
with this music
in this peaceful
    still
    life

Born and raised in Illinois, **Jane Ebihara** has lived in New Jersey since 1977. After receiving a BS from Western Illinois University and an MS from Rutgers University, Jane taught middle school literature in Roxbury, NJ for twenty-six years. As a result of a workshop for teachers sponsored by the Geraldine Dodge Foundation, Jane received a fellowship to the Fine Arts Work Center in Provincetown, MA and also began a poetry group of fellow female teacher/poets who have now been meeting monthly for over twenty years.

Jane has been a volunteer writer for New Jersey NORWESCAP's Senior Life Story Project, and a featured reader in several New Jersey venues. She is the author of *A Little Piece of Mourning* (Finishing Line Press, 2014), and her poems have appeared in many journals and anthologies including *Adanna Literary Journal, Tiferet, U.S. 1 Worksheets, Sonic Boom, The Stillwater Review, The Doll Collection* and *Voices From Here.*

The poems in this chapbook reflect on the quiet moments one finds for reminiscence, rejoicing and regret. They wrestle with loss and longing—those constant companions of the living.

www.ingramcontent.com/pod-product-compliance
Lightning Source LLC
LaVergne TN
LVHW041506070426
835507LV00012B/1352